Guess Who's...
Furry!

Picture credits
(t=top, b=bottom, l=left, r=right, c=centre, fc=front cover)
FLPA: 7, 18 Mark Lane, 10–11 Elliott Neep, 12–13 Thomas Marent/Minden Pictures
Nature PL: 3, 14–15 Steven Kazlowski, 5 Dave Watts, 8–9, 16bl Edwin Griesbers,
Shutterstock: 17tl hironai, 17tc Stayer, 17tr, 17bc, 17br, 19 Eric Isselee, 17bl Igor Kovalchuk,
20 Lorraine Logan

Editor: Alexandra Koken

Copyright © QED Publishing 2012

First published in the UK in 2012 by
QED Publishing
A Quarto Group company
230 City Road
London EC1V 2TT

www.qed-publishing.co.uk

A catalogue record for this book is available from the British Library.

ISBN 978 1 84835 840 9

Printed in China

Guess Who's...

Furry!

Camilla de la Bédoyère and Fiona Hajée

QED Publishing

Who loves
to sleep?

Who has a
furry pouch?

I do!
I am a koala.

When my baby was born, I kept
it safe and warm in my pouch.

Who is covered
with silky
smooth fur?

Who has black and white fur?

Who lives in a forest in China?

Who loves
to eat
bamboo?

Who has long
whiskers?

I do!
I am an
orang-utan.

Who is big
and strong?

Who is asleep in their
den all winter long?

Who is playing
in the snow?

Are you furry?

This orang-utan has spiky orange hair on his head.

What colour is the hair on your head? Is it spiky, straight, wavy or curly?

What names do we give to the hair on our eyelids, above our eyes, and on men's chins?

Whose baby?

Can you match each furry
animal to its baby?

Hungry Molly

Molly the mouse eats lots of different foods.

Count the blackthorn berries.

Count the blackberries.

Count the leaves.

Talking points

The first time you read the book together, encourage your child to guess the identity of each animal before turning the flap. Talk together about how they guessed the animal's identity. Did they look at the picture, listen to the words, or use both sets of clues?

The second time you read the book together, encourage your child to read along with you, especially the repeated words and phrases, such as 'Who...', 'I do' and 'I am'.

Most mammals protect and care for their young. Show your child pictures of themselves as a baby. Talk about how you have looked after them, how they have changed and what they can do now that they couldn't do as a baby.